Get Rid Of The Hurt

A Book About Grieving

By
Madeleine Brehm
and
Rachel Wenzlaff

Children illustrations by David L. Brehm

GET RID OF THE HURT

10-DIGIT ISBN: 1-57543-152-1
13-DIGIT ISBN: 978-1-57543-152-9

REPRINTED 2010
COPYRIGHT © 2007 MAR*CO PRODUCTS, INC.
Published by mar*co products, inc.
1443 Old York Road
Warminster, PA 18974
1-800-448-2197
www.marcoproducts.com

PERMISSION TO REPRODUCE: The purchaser may reproduce the activity sheets, free and without special permission, for participant use for a particular group or class. Reproduction of these materials for an entire school system is forbidden.

All rights reserved. Except as provided above, no part of this book may be reproduced or transmitted in whole or in part in any form or by any means, electronic or mechanical, including photocopying, recording, or by any information storage or retrieval system without permission in writing by the publisher.

Introduction

The loss of a loved one evokes some of our most powerful emotions. The intensity of grief cuts into our hearts. We might like to get rid of the pain, but the hurt won't heal unless we pay attention to it. *Get Rid Of The Hurt* was written to help children find ways to grieve.

Grief is a way to praise and honor the one who has died. Grief helps us take a new look at the future and what our lives will be like without our loved one. All our emotions help us accomplish that, whether we shed tears openly or more quietly, express anger, fear, or physical exhaustion. There are no right or wrong ways to grieve.

Loss may have destroyed—or at least changed—the balance of your life. Don't worry if you feel sad or scared. You're doing the work of grieving and learning to face life in a new way. Grief can't be rushed and can't be fit into a time frame or schedule. The closer you were to the person who has died, the harder it will be to put your grief to rest.

We wrote *Get Rid Of The Hurt* to help you through your sorrow. Grief hurts, but grieving helps us stay physically and emotionally healthy. Grieving will help you discover your own potential and prepare you to pursue your future. Grieve in whatever way feels right to you: Draw, cry, sleep, play games, write, or do whatever makes you feel stronger and more at peace. Then do it over and over again. You'll get rid of the hurt, but you won't lose the love.

How To Use "Get Rid Of The Hurt"

Get Rid Of The Hurt can be used in small-group counseling, individual counseling, or classroom guidance classes. Every child experiences some level of loss. It might be through divorce; the death of a family member, friend, or pet; an accident or fire; unemployment; or the loss or theft of an opportunity or a possession. Everyone experiences some level of pain.

Read this book slowly. Give the children time to process each part. Let the children be your guides as you read. Wait for them to tell you to turn each page. Some pages will be easy for them to hear. Take time with the pages on which the children are doing the work of grieving. Let the children share their experiences and feelings. Doing so helps them get rid of some of the hurt. It takes time for children to look at how life has changed and to get used to the idea that the life they knew has ended. Have paper on hand in case the children want to draw. Be ready if they want to take a walk or play a game. Stand next to a child who needs to cry, offering comfort and support. Find a safe place for the children to cry or release their anger. We are the children's guides, but we must let them lead the way. Children will want to read some pages over and over. There are some pages you'll have to read only once, because the children have completed their grieving work in the areas those pages describe. Don't be afraid to ask, "Is this a grieving day?" as you begin a group. And don't be surprised if you can sometimes answer that question without asking it. There will be days when the answer will be evident in how the children look or behave or in what they say. Don't be afraid to share your own grief. Children will learn that grief comes to all of us and that we all have to learn ways to get rid of the hurt.

Personalizing "Get Rid Of The Hurt"

You may want to give each child a copy of the entire story (pages 7-46) or distribute selected pages for each child to personalize. If this idea appeals to you, reproduce whatever content you feel is appropriate for the child in question. Allow him/her to create a personal book. This memento will serve as a valuable touchstone when the child is away from the counseling environment.

ASCA Standards For "Get Rid Of The Hurt"

ACADEMIC DEVELOPMENT

Standard A: Students will acquire the attitudes, knowledge and skills that contribute to effective learning in school and across the life span.

A:A3	Achieve School Success
A:A3.1	Take responsibility for their actions

PERSONAL/SOCIAL DEVELOPMENT

Standard A: Students will acquire the knowledge, attitudes and interpersonal skills to help them understand and respect self and others.

PS:A1	Acquire Self-Knowledge
PS:A1.2	Identify values, attitudes and beliefs
PS:A1.4	Understand change is a part of growth
PS:A1.6	Distinguish between appropriate and inappropriate behavior
PS:A1.8	Understand the need for self-control and how to practice it
PS:A1.10	Identify personal strengths and assets
PS:A2	Acquire Interpersonal Skills
PS:A2.5	Recognize and respect differences in various family configurations
PS:A2.6	Use effective communications skills

Standard B: Students will make decisions, set goals and take necessary action to achieve goals.

PS:B1	Self-Knowledge Application
PS:B1.2	Understand consequences of decisions and choices
PS:B1.3	Identify alternative solutions to a problem
PS:B1.5	Demonstrate when, where and how to seek help for solving problems and making decisions
PS:B1.11	Use persistence and perseverance in acquiring knowledge and skills

American School Counselor Association (2004). ASCA National Standards for Students. Alexandria, VA: © 2004 by the American School Counselor Association

Get Rid Of The Hurt

What Is  Grieving?

When you lose someone you love, you feel sad. Grieving is whatever you do to express the pain.

Circle each of the ways you let your pain out.
Add any others that are not on the page.

Screaming

Running

Sleeping

Crying

Exercising

Drawing

If you do not grieve, everything gets stuck inside.

When you grieve, you feel better.

Let the tears flow.

Take a walk.

Think.

Take some deep breaths.

Hug your favorite stuffed animal.

DRAWING

is a great way to express yourself and get rid of your hurt.

Draw a picture of the loved one you lost doing what you liked doing with him or her.

Draw a picture of your family.

Draw your favorite holiday or favorite kind of weather.

Draw a picture on this page that will help you get rid of your hurt.

Start a memory book.

What do you remember about your loved one?

Color of eyes _____

Color of hair _____

Height _____

Type of job _____

Number of children _____

Birthplace _____

Hobbies _____

Musical instrument(s) played _____

Loved one's special name for you _____

Your favorite name for your loved one _____

Places you went together _____

Where your loved one lived _____

Favorite gift you gave your loved one _____

Favorite gift your loved one gave you _____

If you wish, you may make a small book and title it **My Memory Book Of** _____. Take the information from the sentences above and divide it into pages. Illustrate the pages, staple them together, and you'll have a loving keepsake of someone who was very important to you.

There's a new space in your life ready to be filled.

Draw a line under each activity you will use to fill that space.

Play sports.
Read books.
Have fun.
Draw.
Join a club.
Play videogames.
Study.
Dance.
Play an instrument.
Work hard.
Make new friends.
Write stories.
Take a grieving class.
Learn to cook.
Exercise.
Get a pet or train your pet.
Sing.

If you don't let the pain out, you might:

get sick.
have a stomachache.
have a headache.
feel tired all the time.

Your sad feelings are very important.

Share them with a counselor, teacher, parent, friend, family member, or anyone you can trust.

Make a list of everyone you trust to share
your feelings and why you trust each person.

_____

_____

_____

_____

Make a list of people with who you will not share this loss and
why you won't share your feelings with these people.

_____

_____

_____

Practice saying aloud the **FEELING** words, then complete the following sentences:

You may think:

My life will be different.
People will treat me differently.
I will be left out.
I will have no future.
I can't concentrate on my schoolwork.

What other thoughts have you had or might you have?
Write them on the lines below:

_____

_____

_____

_____

Your future will always be the life you choose to create.

What will help you get on with your life?

Circle each thing that will help you get on with your life.
Add anything that is not listed below.

Pets

Friends

Family

Religion

Clubs

Music

Sports

School

_____

_____

_____

Positive self-talk
is saying things to yourself that make you feel better.

Things like:

I'm going to be OK!

Think of some other things you could say to yourself that would help you believe in yourself and feel better.
Write those things on the lines below:

_____

_____

_____

_____

Send some good wishes to your loved one!

I hope my _____ is having a good time.

I hope my _____ .

I wish _____ .

I want_____ .

I want to say _____ .

I want to say,

I love you and miss you.

I send hugs and kisses to my loved one every day and at night when I go to bed.

This is a picture of me in bed sending hugs and kisses to:

_____

Don't take your feelings out
on yourself or on anyone else.
It's OK to feel whatever you are feeling.

All feelings are OK.

It's what you do with your feelings
that makes them good or bad.

There is no right or wrong way to grieve.

It is OK to share your feelings with your diary,
your pet, or your favorite stuffed animal.

You may grieve by crying out loud.

Or you may grieve silently to yourself while
hugging your pet or a pillow
or just walking from room to room in your home.

Telling others what happened to our loved one may make us feel better.

Share what happened with everyone you trust.
People want to hear your story.

Share it!
Share it!
Share it!

What happened?

_____

_____

_____

_____

_____

_____

Grieving takes a lot of ENERGY.

After a loss, you'll get tired easily.

You'll need lots of rest.

Your chest and shoulders might hurt or feel heavy.

Exercise will be good for you at this time.

Eating right is very important while you are grieving.

Remind your parents to put healthful foods into your body.

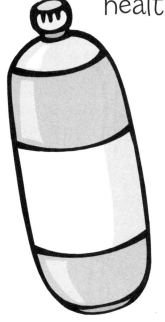

Drink lots of water.

Use less sugar.

What else can you do to stay healthy?

_____
_____
_____
_____

The pain of grieving may flare up at any time, even when you are on the way to school.

All of a sudden, you'll have tears in your eyes and you won't be sure what made you want to cry.

Was it the words of a song?
Was it a picture you saw?
Or something that caught your eye while you were looking out the window?

It's OK to feel this way.
These feelings are normal and lots of kids and adults have them.
These quiet tears are your way of saying hello to your loved one and showing how much you miss him or her.

A funeral is a service to celebrate, say goodbye, and share memories and feelings about someone who has died.

Your parents will help you decide whether you should go to your loved one's funeral. Share your thoughts with your parents. Tell them how you feel about going to the funeral:

I would like (wanted) to go to the funeral because ...

_____

_____

_____

I do (did) not want to go to the funeral because ...

_____

_____

_____

Some kids do not want to go to a loved one's funeral.

Place a check in the box next to each thought that applies to you.

☐ Not everyone wants to attend the funeral.

☐ Hearing people talk about your loved one makes you sad.

☐ You do not want to think about the fact that your loved one has died.

☐ You do not want to remember your loved one in a casket.

☐ You may not want people telling you how sorry they are.

☐ You do not like people handing you sympathy cards.

☐ You do not want people to feel sorry for you.

☐ You want to think about what a great life you had with your loved one.

Some kids want to go to a loved one's funeral.

Place a check in the box next to each thought that applies to you.

☐ You are old enough to go to the funeral.

☐ You want to go to the funeral and your parents want you to go.

☐ You want to see your loved one's friends and relatives.

☐ You want to hear the positive stories people are going to tell about your loved one.

☐ You want to share your own stories about your loved one.

You will not grieve every day.

Answer each statement by circling Yes or No.

Today is a grieving day.   Yes   No

Today is not a grieving day.   Yes   No

Think about each day of the week. Which days are usually grieving days for you and which are usually not grieving days?

Circle the answer that is most correct for you.

Sunday	Yes	No
Monday	Yes	No
Tuesday	Yes	No
Wednesday	Yes	No
Thursday	Yes	No
Friday	Yes	No
Saturday	Yes	No

If today is a grieving day, circle each activity that feels right for you to do.

If today is not a grieving day, underline each activity that would have felt right for you to do on your last grieving day.

Cry.
Sit and stare.
Draw a picture of your loved one.
Look at pictures of your loved one.
Think of happy times you shared with your loved one.
Take five deep breaths.
Think of a favorite gift your loved one gave you.
Think of a favorite gift you gave your loved one.
Think of something your loved one taught you.
Listen to music.
Call a friend to talk about your loved one.
Ride a bike.
Play with your pet.
Take a nap.
Play a sport.
Have a sleepover.
Play a videogame.
Read a book.
Do your homework.

On the following lines, list any activities that are not included above.

_____

_____

_____

Something good can sometimes result from losing a loved one.

If your loved one was ill, there will be no more suffering.

Think about your loved one.

On the lines below, list what good things might come out of this sad event.

_____

_____

_____

_____

Your loved one is not with you physically,

but he or she can be in your thoughts wherever you go.

You can always talk or write to your loved one.

In fact, now is a good time to write in your diary what you would like to say to your loved one.

Dear Diary,

_____

_____

_____

_____

_____

Love you,

Think about ways your life has changed.

Then write the answer to the following question on the lines below.

How is my life different since my loved one passed away?

_____

_____

_____

_____

_____

_____

_____

_____

Think about ways your life has not changed.
Then write the answer to the following question on the lines below.

How is my life the same?

_____
_____
_____
_____
_____
_____
_____

Grieving will not last forever.

Things will get better!

I feel sad now, but I won't always feel sad.

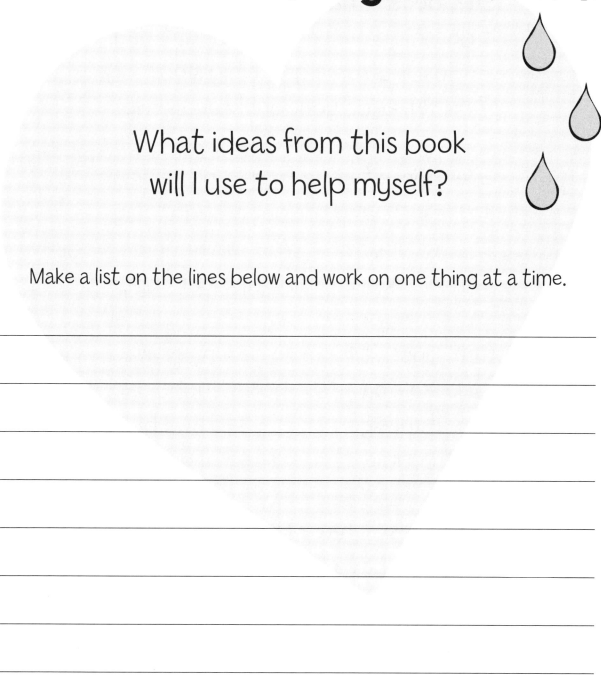

What ideas from this book
will I use to help myself?

Make a list on the lines below and work on one thing at a time.

_____

_____

_____

_____

_____

_____

_____

_____

Grief doesn't have to get in the way.
It doesn't have to spoil a bright day.
Just put on a great big smile,
And set aside your grief for a while.

Grief doesn't have to get in the way.
It doesn't have to spoil a bright day.
Just put on a nice, wide grin
And work on holding up your chin.

Grief doesn't have to get in the way.
It doesn't have to spoil a bright day.
Sometimes you will feel sad and blue.
But in time, those days will be few.

Grief doesn't have to get in the way.
It doesn't have to spoil a bright day.
Just keep a smile on your face
And tell Grief, "Get off my case."

 Rachel Wenzlaff

 Madeleine Brehm

Empowering children and adults is one of my most enduring aspirations. If children can look at their lives and see their uniqueness and what they can share with themselves and others, their personal power can blossom. We all affect each other every day. The way and extent to which we help, encourage, and support others is tested every day. Some days, we are great. Some days, we're not so great.

I've been an elementary school counselor for 23 years. I've taught parenting classes and run small groups and individual counseling sessions. But the sudden death of my husband challenged my belief in my personal power. Everything I had taught about facing life's challenges came back to me and I had to answer and face the impact of grief. Knowledge is power, but life experiences touch the heart. When that happens, we can regain possession of our personal power only by digging deep within ourselves to empower our lives. My hope is that *Get Rid Of The Hurt* will help you find peace and power.

Rachel Wenzlaff

This is Rachel Wenzlaff's first book. Born on August 19, 1994, she lost her father when she was 9 years old. Rachel has a mother, an annoying little brother, and two wonderful dogs. She's obsessed with cheerleading and the swim team. When she isn't at school, she's involved in some sports activity somewhere. Rachel's favorite subject is English. She's a straight-A student who hopes to keep her place on the Honor Roll. She wants to earn a scholarship to the University of Texas, where she plans to study marketing or real estate. She wants to marry at 25 and die when she is very, very old. When she does die, Rachel wants to be buried with her family.